How To Master
Your IPad 3

In-Depth Guide To Jail Breaking Apps,

Features And Exclusive Secrets

By: Don Gall

TABLE OF CONTENTS

Publishers Notes

Disclaimer

This publication is intended to provide helpful and informative material. It is not intended to diagnose, treat, cure, or prevent any health problem or condition, nor is intended to replace the advice of a physician. No action should be taken solely on the contents of this book. Always consult your physician or qualified health-care professional on any matters regarding your health and before adopting any suggestions in this book or drawing inferences from it.

The author and publisher specifically disclaim all responsibility for any liability, loss or risk, personal or otherwise, which is incurred as a consequence, directly or indirectly, from the use or application of any contents of this book.

Any and all product names referenced within this book are the trademarks of their respective owners. None of these owners have sponsored, authorized, endorsed, or approved this book.

Always read all information provided by the manufacturers' product labels before using their products. The author and publisher are not responsible for claims made by manufacturers.

Paperback Edition 2013

Manufactured in the United States of America

DEDICATION

This book is dedicated to Estelle. The information she provided was essential in the collation of this text.

INTRODUCTION

The iPad3 has the ability to stream movies, to play great games and has thousands of apps available in the Apple App Store. There are a lot of great uses for the iPad3.

Just who would be the kind of user who would get the most out of an iPad? Well those who travel around quite a lot would certainly find an iPad to be the perfect companion. With the option of 3G connectivity, an iPad would be great with both productivity as well as be a source of entertainment. The iPad3 provides the perfect way to surf the web at home as is also an excellent eReader, with the ability to read eBooks from Apple's iBooks, Amazon's Kindle and Barnes and Noble's Nook.

Between its ability to hit Facebook, read Email and being able to browse the web, the iPad3 can replace the laptop for many people who may not take to more traditional computers. Just about anyone in business could make good use of the iPad's thousands of business apps. In fact so many industries have come to see the iPad as a new way of computing. Musicians find they can take full advantage of a lot of helpful apps that range from a digital piano to a guitar effects processor.

Many people tend to think that the iPad is just another expensive toy, however that description wouldn't do it justice The iPad is so much more than that. Apple's new technological gadget is a mobile computer and is considered quite revolutionary since it is neither a laptop or a personal digital assistant.

No doubt many may have decided to purchase an iPad due to all of the recent media buzz and aggressive marketing. For many newbies and others who are not serious techies may not consider the pros and cons of the iPad right now but what they want to know is, just what is an iPad and what can it do?

The iPad is mainly designed for the consumption of information though Web browsing, media, and gaming. In addition, it can be also be used to create documents and other kinds of content on a lighter level. The iPad is powered by thousands of apps that permit it to perform at a fast speed .

The iPad was a quite a big hit when it first arrived on the market and it continues to amaze even the most jaded of consumers. Expect Apple to release newer models over time. They have been successful in creating a model and bring about enhancements that are intended to adapt to consumer's everyday lives. Perhaps in the future the newer iPads will either get bigger, or even smaller. One thing to expect is that Apple will continue to amaze and will plan on releasing a fast, easy-to-use iPad for years to come.

CHAPTER 1- THE iPAD- YET ANOTHER OF EXAMPLE OF APPLE'S INNOVATION STRATEGY

Apple has put together an Innovation Factory – a factory that encourages and harnesses unbridled creativity from its people. Apple does this by coming up with stimulating bold & enterprising new ideas, and launching successful, profitable new innovations like the iPad.

iPad is a Tablet type of computer that is made up of a flat touch screen which can use a digital pen, fingertips or a stylus. It is being marketed precisely to provide a solution to the problems of viewing movies, or be able to read the web content or articles, periodicals, games and also music.

The operating system of the iPod touch and the iPhone are very similar to the operating system of the iPad. It can run the applications of the iPhone and do it as well as running its self developed precise applications. Without any modifications (or Jailbreaking) being made only the programs which are being approved of by Apple and which are currently being distributed through Apple's online can be run on the iPad. In a way that is similar to the iPod touch and iPhone it is also controlled by the multitouch display which makes the iPad head and shoulders above the older tablet computers which still use a pressure triggered stylus.

The iPad's mobile data connection is Wi-Fi or 3G which enables it to connect to the internet and then even more important to be able to browse, load, stream the media and then installing of the software. It is made with a dock connector for be able to have the wired connectivity but at the same time it lacks the presence of USB ports and Ethernet that are found on the large computers. It also has an built-in Bluetooth 2.1+EDR that makes it appear to be more stylish due to the fact that it is possible to connect the earphones and the keyboard to it without any necessary wires. The synchronization and management of the iPad is done by iTunes via USB on a personal computer.

The media has given some really positive reviews to this new exciting and promising creation of Apple! The Apple iPad is considered one of the hottest selling articles in recent years because of its unique and salient features which make it stand at least a class apart from most other gadgets.

CHAPTER 2- WHAT EXACTLY MAKES THE IPAD 3 DIFFERENT FROM OTHER IPAD VERSIONS?

Evolution of the iPad

Apple has been pleasing consumers for many years with their innovative and stylish electronic items. They blew up the music industry with their signature iPods and have allowed consumers to enjoy their favorite tunes wherever they go at low cost as well as providing a convenient, portable item. One of the newest creations of Apple is in the form of a tablet, which was an electronic device that is easily portable and offers touch-screen usage for easy navigation and convenience. The iPad is also host to a wealth of entertainment through a variety of specifically designed applications, giving users a world of access to their favorite entertainment as well as work oriented communication. The iPad first burst onto the scene in 2010 with their first model, the original iPad, and have been making improvements ever since.

The first iPad came out in January of 2010. The world was in shock and awe at how incredible this device looked at first; it was the size of a laptop, but the convenience and portability of a large Smartphone. Offering a 9.7 inch touch-screen display, the iPad was a breath of fresh air in the world of electronics. Some felt that the item was much too big to be carried around, but as sales noted, it was a big hit. Stores were selling out everywhere and people couldn't get enough of the iPad. It has an Apple A4 processor at its core and displayed images at a beautiful 1,024x768 resolution. The iPad also ran off Apple's iOS 5.1.a operating system, giving it all the great Apple features and controls Apple consumers are already used to. It offered a handful of wireless features like Wi-Fi connectivity and Bluetooth 2.1 options. This added to the convenience and wireless attraction. With 256 MD of RAM, the applications ran smoothly and effortlessly.

Another interesting aspect for the first iPad was the 3G cellular option. Much like a cell phone, having 3G would allow you to have internet access without the need for connecting to Wi-Fi. This would be activated with a monthly fee.

As always, technology advances and become better. Apple introduced their new iPad 2 on March of 2011. They kept the same screen size, 9.7 inches, as well as the resolution size. What did change, however, was the internal processor, getting upped to an Apple A5 chip. There was even a small boost to the CPU power as well as doubling the RAM size. What really activated this change were the huge amounts of new applications that hit the market. Some more advanced than others. In order to run them effectively, Apple needed to enhance their machine to give it that extra performance boost.

The iPad 2 is really where applications and application makers reached for the stars. Many new complex games came out that took advantage of the touch-screen features. Adventure games had crisper graphics as well as precise control. This is also why Apple added a gyroscope to the iPad. Games can now be controlled by simply tilting the tablet to the left or right, adding extra control.

Another year passes and another tablet is released. Apple likes to "surprise" consumers with a new model of their hottest item 12-18 months in between. This is what led to the unveiling of the iPad 3. Becoming a bigger item than their first tablet, the iPad 3 added a whole new level of clarity in the touch screen.

The biggest change was taking their iPad from the resolution of 1,024x768 and upped the game to 2,048x1536 pixels with a 264ppi. This new change is called "Retina Display" which amazes consumers and tech critics alike. This big jump in visuals brings even more application manufacturers as they produce console-quality gaming experiences. The retina display also touts the e-book world as a way to replace your older e-book reader. The crisp lines, the incredible contrast gives consumers the feeling that they are reading something that looks even sharper than if they were reading an actual book. After a consumer has downloaded their favorite e-book reading application, they can keep a library of their favorite books for easy accessibility.

With the added Retina Display technology, comic book companies jumped at the chance to present consumers their comics in digital versions. The display was exceptional for representing the small text as well as the vibrant colors of typical comic books. Comic fans were enthusiastic at the change, giving them instant access to the newest titles and a library to store everything when they need them.

Of course with the image enhancements, also come the advancements in power. The iPad 3 really ups its game by bringing in the new Apple A5X chip that moves even faster and smoother than both its predecessors. The RAM even gets doubled to handle all the new applications to the iPad 3 boasts a total of 1024 MB of Ram for incredible performance.

The iPad 3 still holds the same screen size, coming in at 9.7 like the other two before it. There is still great Wi-Fi connectivity to surf the internet at home, or wherever there is a wireless signal. What also stayed was the 3G connectivity, but it was enhanced with LET on 4G models. This offered faster download speeds giving consumers better access to streaming media. The weight of the iPad 3 increased a little bit since the iPad 2, but that's only because of the upped memory and enhances power. It's definitely a small sacrifice to enjoy this super-fast, incredible technology.

The iPad 3 can support features that allow users to customize it according to their particular needs. For the business user, they will have more space to store their data. They would benefit from a device that can be easily carried around and also be a powerful tool that they can use to control their vast businesses right in the palm of their hand. They would want supporting software to assist them in making important business decisions thought decision making systems software and similar other stuff.

IPad is a revolutionary product with its wafer thin frame and a 9.7 inch screen has taken over the market for wireless computing devices. The iPad comes in models which allow connectivity to the internet and come in the WIFI and the 3G versions. The iPad uses a lithium battery which has a long shelf life. The device is very easy to carry around. There are a lot of applications which can be added to the existing fleet of applications being used in the iPad 3.

Chapter 3- What Exactly Is Jailbreaking For The iPad 3?

The term 'Jailbreaking for the iPad 3' means to free the piece of hardware from all or some of its restrictions that Apple has put in place. This is a common practice for software companies to control their products and gain revenue so consumers that purchase their brand of hardware can only use applications that are specifically designed under Apple's direction. There are many individuals who are opposed to this form of limitation and shop around for jailbreaking software for their mobile devices.

Jailbreaking software enables the user to use the features that can be of valuable resource to them while they are traveling for work or personal ventures. The freedom to be able to use applications they are accustomed to using can help with business meetings or something as simple as playing one's favorite games while waiting for their flight or passing the time during their daily commute on the train.

Once jailbreak has freed up the iPad 3 there are a multitude of applications that are available to the consumer. Many consumers like the idea of being able to control what goes on their mobile devices and customization is one of the major advantages of jailbreaking. There are many different nifty features with jailbreaking applications like the lock screen feature, slide bar as well as the music player which can be altered to anything the consumer would like to have on their screen. Many technical geeks love being able to manipulate their devices so they can have their favorite games, music or photos ready and available when and where they want it on their devices without limitations.

A great advantage for those who want to try jailbreaking for the iPad 3 is how easily it can be done. In a matter of a few minutes the application can be completed and if it is not well suited can also be reversed just as quickly. Most consumers rarely take this step and love the capabilities they are given with jailbreaking but it is nice to know that there are options available should one want to make that change.

There are some dream applications like Cydia, Dreamboard and MyWi that enables the user to 'tether' one's mobile device with a USB cable to gain access to the internet. This can be a very important feature for those who are always on the move and need to be able to access the internet without the higher costs of a data plan. These kinds of applications can also help with downloading files, movies, pictures as well as graphs and spreadsheets in a jiffy. There are a lot of popular applications like Tetris that are completely free of charge. Wallpapers, designer icons and lifetime memberships can all be part of the great package that one receives with their jailbreaking software.

Certainly there are always pro's and con's to every application change and jailbreaking is no exception. One of the things to never do when one has applied the jailbreaking application is to download updates from Apple as it will totally wipe out the jailbreak application and cause applications to immediately stop working. The key to avoiding this is to ensure that there is an available jailbreak application to fix this prior to installing updates if the individual were interested in downloading the current updates.

There can also be some applications that will crash more often as well as a bigger consumption of battery life. Apple also will not back up the warranty should they find that jailbreaking software has been used but the way to handle that would be to 'restore' the device back to its original settings in iTunes and it will appear like it's never seen a jailbreaking application. It is also highly advisable to back up one's devices prior to any new installation just in case something should go wrong.

The search for a great jailbreaking application for the iPad 3 can be done on the internet quite quickly. There are lots of available vendors that offer this type of service and selecting the right one takes a little bit of research. This very crucial step should be taken as to prevent viruses, Trojan horses or pure scams that could end up destroying or wiping out one's mobile device. One of the safest ways to jailbreak one's mobile device is to take it to a reputable developer who has the expertise to perform this type of service and in some cases will even replace the iPad 3 if damage should come during the installation process. There is of course a nominal fee that is involved with professional services like these but if the individual were not comfortable with loading this software on to their device this might be the way to go. In general some jailbreaking software is free of charge but most websites will ask for some sort of donation for their services on jailbreaking software for their iPad 3. For some individuals this is the type of service that is appealing to them while others like to install these kinds of software on their own. The choice is really a personal preference and how comfortable they are with downloading an application and how much research one is willing to invest to purchase this kind of software.

A trustworthy vendor will be able to provide unlimited support on installation, troubleshooting or removal of their application. Most will offer a 30 day money back guarantee if the individual is experiencing issues. The software should also be very easy to understand even for the first time user who have never installed an application on their devices before.

Some of these applications will come with a multiple use type of jailbreaking. For example it can include jailbreaking software for the iPad 3 but also for the iPhone or iPod as well. When researching for these kinds of applications make sure that you have the right versions of your mobile devices as some of these can cater to specific versions only. While there are other applications that work regardless of what version of mobile device one has. It is also vital that the software be totally reversible so the individual can still make use of their Apple warranty.

CHAPTER 4- WHY WOULD ANYONE CHOSE TO JAILBREAK THE IPAD 3?

For many people the main reason to jailbreak an iPad is to be able to multitask, which means the ability to manage several applications at the same time without having to close them first By using Backgrounder.

Another great reason to jailbreak your iPad is great theme utility called Winterboard. This utility allows users to use any image as the iPad's background image instead of on the lock screen as it would be done on the iPhone.

One your device is jailbroken there is a whole host of modifications and customization that can are possible. These include:

• Being able to control your iPad3 from your computer By using VNC server

- It will be possible to turn your iPad3 into a hotspot - Internet Tether

- The ability to play any video file format on your iPad by using vlc4iPhone

- Be able to take advantage of your 3g connection with other devices by using MyWi

- Access to thousands of banned, restricted Apps By using Installous, Cydia and Rock

- Synchronize your iPad3 with your iTunes account with WiFi By using WiFi Sync

- You can now play flash content By using Skyfire web browser, Cloud browse, ISwifter on your device.

- Customize the appearance of your iPad3's springboard

An important thing to consider is that it will be Apple's policy that jailbreaking your device voids your warranty and it can take some time and effort jailbreaking your device.

CHAPTER 5- HOW TO JAILBREAK THE IPAD 3

There are a great many sources that claim to have the capability or resources to jailbreak an iPad 3. It is important to make sure that the resource that is selected is indeed capable of performing the task for which it is intended. The first thing you will need to do will be to ensure that the resource you select is indeed legitimate. There are also many sources out there that will claim to have the capability to jailbreak your device only to end up charging without delivering the desired results. That said, it is probably better to have your device jail broken by a professional for a fee rather than use a free service with which you are unfamiliar. One of the major benefits of doing so, is that professionals will likely use methods that are well tested and verified.

While there is no absolute guarantee that a jail broken device will work, working with a professional will at least provide you with some recourse in the event that the process does not work as intended. Should you decide to do this on your own, it will be important to make sure that you download the software that is compatible to your computer as well as to the version of your iPad. Fortunately, jailbreaking is no longer as daunting a task as it used to be. It is significantly simpler than it was in the past. This is a result of the availability of a variety of tools that have been designed to function in a much more user friendly fashion than before.

If you have an IPad 3 5.1 and decide to opt for an untethered jailbreak, one of the available methods is through the software package known as Absinthe. It will be necessary to download the Absinthe package that is appropriate for your computer. You will want to make sure that the software is downloaded from a reputable website. There are software versions available for both Macintosh computers as well as Windows PCs. After the download has been completed, you will notice a new folder on your desktop. The folder will most likely have an Absinthe related title. It will then be necessary to extract the files from the folder prior to launching Absinthe.

After all the files are extracted, you will then need to launch Absinthe. Prior to launching Absinthe, you will also want to disable any passwords on your tablet. Failure to do so may cause the process to fail. Once the software is launched, you will then be prompted to connect your device to the computer. As the software progresses with the jailbreak, you will receive a variety of updates. The software will then reboot your device. After the device is rebooted you should receive a message informing you that the process was a success. If the jailbreak process was successful, users will notice a Cydia icon on the home screen of their tablet. This application will be used to locate and download applications that were previously inaccessible on the device that is not jail broken.

It is important to note that there are periodic updates to the Absinthe jailbreak software. What this means for users, is that the process should be conducted at a user's own risk as the updates clearly indicate that there is work yet to be done to perfect the process. Jailbreaking the device on one's own can still prove to be tricky and at worst unsuccessful. The safest way how to go about getting the job done is by having it completed by someone with expert knowledge of the process. Doing so has several benefits such as the availability of access to support in the event that the device malfunctions.

Users can also jailbreak their IPads using Redsn0w. Redsn0w is an alternative software program which will also need to be downloaded to your computer system. Once you download Redsn0w, it will then need to be unzipped and run on your computer. The software will then reside on your computer where it can then be used in the jailbreak process. The user will then need to connect their IPad to their computer system and turn it off. After the IPad is turned off, the user will then need to choose the "install Cydia" option in the software program. Before going any further in the process, it will be necessary to put your IPad into what is referred to as "DFU mode". If you are unaware of how to go about putting the device into this state mode, please refer to the instructions below.

Steps to get to DFU mode

It is important to have the latest ITunes software installed on your computer. In order to get into DFU mode, You will first need to hold your power button for approximately 5 seconds. While still holding the power button, you will then need to press the home button for approximately 10 seconds. It is important not to let go of either button during this process. You will then need to let go of the power button while you continue to keep your finger on the home button for approximately 15 seconds. This process may require a couple of attempts to achieve success. Once successful, you will be prompted accordingly by the iTunes software on your computer.

After the device is successfully in DFU mode, the Redsn0w software program will automatically process the jailbreak of your device. If the process is successful, the next screen you encounter on the software program will prompt you to install Cydia. You will then need to press the "next" button in order to successfully install the application. Upon a successful jailbreak, you will receive a prompt on your screen notifying you that the jailbreak process has been completed successfully. It will then be necessary to reboot your device in order to complete the process.

It is always advisable to back up the contents of your device prior to jailbreaking it. This creates a point to which you can restore the device if the jailbreak is unsuccessful. It is also important to note that jailbreaking a device will effectively void any contract that you have through Apple.

Chapter 6- How Does One Hack the iPad 3?

While an untethered hack for the iPad 3 has just recently been announced, that doesn't mean that one can't take the preliminary steps necessary to prepare for hacking the device. However, the official release of the evasi0n software has been rumored by some that it will be released this coming Sunday, February 3rd. In order to hack the iPad 3, one can set up software on their computer to jailbreak their iPad. Afterwards, they can install homebrew applications, homebrew games, and emulators and even load movie and music collections onto their device. There have been some that have claimed to have already hacked the iPad 3 iOS 6.1 and have produced a working jailbreaking exploit known as Absinthe 2.0. However, this jailbreaking exploit has been claimed by some to be false and may also contain malware viruses that can infect a user's computer.

Before one can begin hacking their iPad, they will need to obtain a 30-pin to USB cable, the evasi0n software for iOS 6.x and a compatible computer system with an available USB port. The computer systems that are compatible with the evasi0n software include Windows operating systems with at least Windows XP, Macintosh systems operating on at least 10.5 OSX and Linux operating systems operating on a x86 / x86_64 system core.

After connecting the iPad 3 to a compatible computer system with the 30-pin to USB cable, the person may wait a moment for iTunes to recognize that the device has been connected. It is recommended that the user update their iTunes version to at least version 10.7 with an iOS 6.1 so that all features of the firmware may be taken advantage of alongside the device being hacked. Various firmware features that are installed include important system updates, application patches and even system themes that improve the performance.

It is beneficial for one to ensure that they have updated their firmware to the iOS 6.1 before continuing with the jailbreaking process. When updating the firmware, it is important to download the iOS 6.1 firmware update from the Internet and manually install it through iTunes rather than downloading the iOS 6.1 update over-the-air and updating the iPad 3. After downloading the iOS 6.1 file, it may be installed by opening the iTunes 10.7 applications and clicking on the "Check for Update" button located in the program while simultaneously holding down the Option key if using a Mac or the Shift key if using Windows or Linux PC systems. Upon successfully doing so a message will be displayed and will ask the user to select an update file for iTunes. Once prompted, the user may navigate to the directory location they saved the iOS 6.1 update to and select it. Once selected, the iOS 6.1 update will be installed to the iTunes 10.7 program.

After iTunes has been updated to the appropriate version and iOS 6.1, the user will be able to launch the evasi0n software to jailbreak their iPad 3. Typically the jailbreaking process is automated after it has been initiated and the user will then have the familiar apps on their iPad 3. When the user opens the evasi0n program, the software will auto-recognize the iPad device connected and will then be ready to jailbreak. The evasi0n development team is currently in the process of completing the GUI of the evasion software and once complete private beta testing of the software is scheduled to begin. Once the bugs have been ironed out, the software will then be released.

After jailbreaking an iPad 3, there are multiple things that the user can do with it. There are many useful homebrew applications as well as many user created homebrew games.

There are also emulators that one can load onto their iPad 3 to play classic NES, Super Nintendo, Sega Genesis, Playstation and even Nintendo 64 games. Often, many homebrew games will also include ports of other PC games or console games that are "ported" to work with the iPad 3. Some people may enjoy these homebrew games and emulated games; however there are some tat may enjoy what the homebrew software has to offer more.

Many homebrew applications allow the user to do various things that might enhance the overall system performance or change the basic theme of the iPad. Other useful features of some homebrew apps also allow the user to swap application icons to various types of icon images. Besides the option of changing the theme of the iPad and tweaking system performance, the user may also download homebrew applications to perform other tasks as well.

Other homebrew applications allow the user to install various applications from a homebrew type of store known as Cydia. The Cydia application is also one of the first applications that are installed onto the iPad 3 once it is jail broken with the evasi0n jailbreaking software. Users may also download and install a homebrew application that will allow them access to the Apple store for viewing and obtaining free versions of their apps from alternate links. Besides the many homebrew applications that are available, the system tweaks that one may configure also go further than just changing the theme of the iPad or the icon images. Users may also make custom changes to the springboard of the iOS as well as other system features that allow the user to scroll differently.

So in conclusion, while the Absinthe 2.0 jailbreaking software has been known for some time, it is said by some to be a fake program that does not hack the iPad 3 iOS 6.1 operating system and may in fact harbor harmful viruses. However, the evasi0n jailbreaking software was recently announced and is about to begin private beta testing. Soon after private beta testing has completed, the evasi0n software will be released and users may connect their iPad 3 to a compatible computer to jailbreak it using the evasi0n software. Once they have jail broken their iPad 3, they may load homebrew applications, games, emulators and their collections of multimedia.

CHAPTER 7- WHAT ARE THEMES FOR THE IPAD 3?

When it comes to themes, it is all about actually installing the scenery adjustments to the tablet computer. The Apple iPad 3 is designed to look universal, no matter who is using the equipment or what applications they have on it. Although the applications can change, the overall look of it usually does not, unless a theme is installed. This must be done from an outside source, so although there are a large variety of themes, ranging from everything looking like Star Wars to Barbie, every single icon and background is adjusted in order to adhere to the new theme. In order to use the themes, a theme must be installed onto the iPad 3.

Jailbreaking the iPad 3

Themes are available through an application known as Cydia. Cydia is essentially a third party application source on the Apple iPad and iPhones, which is run outside of the realm of the App Store. These applications do not need to be approved by Apple, and although you're never really sure what you're getting with some of these applications, there are a large number of Themes available here. To start though, you must first Jailbreak your tablet computer. You are in luck, as although congress recently changed regulations to state it is illegal to mod and jailbreak a mobile phone from one carrier to another, it is still legal to jailbreak a tablet computer.

Before you can look at the themes from the iPad 3, you need to install jailbreak software onto your user computer. This includes Blackra1n and Greenpois0n. You just need to navigate to one of these websites and download the application for your Windows or Mac computer. It doesn't take all that long to do so. Once it is downloaded, connect your iPad 3 to your computer and launch the application on the computer. It is automatically going to detect the connected iPad and start the process. Before you jailbreak the tablet you should make sure you have backed up everything to iTunes, because if you don't, you might be completely out of luck. When the jailbreak software begins to run, select to install "Cydia" during the jailbreak process.

After the jailbreak process is complete, it is going to reboot your iPad 3 and launch it. At first, it is going to look exactly the same, but when you scroll through your app icons, you are going to see the "Cydia" icon. Select this icon and allow it to initialize. This takes a few moments, but eventually it is going to close out the application, once it has finished. This is normal, so allow it to do so. After completing the process, select the application again and now you can start using the Application.

Themes for the iPad 3

Type in "Themes" into the Cydia application and you are able to look at the different available themes for you to select from. There are literally hundreds of different application themes available to you, so you need to possibly install different ones in order to see which one you like the best.

Android LS Dream

If you have ever seen some of your friends use a Droid based phone, you might have seen a rather colorful background with the time at the top of the device and the temperature and weather conditions included. This application is rather popular, as you can have your iPad function in a similar way to an Android device, if you like the look.

Bookshelf Theme

If you are all about the magazine and text books available on the iPad 3, this application is for you. The main screen is going to look like an actual wall with several shelves on the back. Your current purchases appear in large image form on the top book shelf, while smaller application icons appear in the bottom, left corner of the screen. In the bottom right, you have a calendar. This gives off the look of a book shelf or a study.

Star Wars Theme

If you are a big fan of Star Wars, you can make your entire iPad 3 reflect this. You are able to change the background image to one you like, and you can even alter the app icons, from a picture of the Death Star to R2-D2. Of course, this is only one of the many different Star Wars themes, as most popular movies do have several different themes available. Star Wars has one of the largest libraries out there, so if you enjoy the movie you are going to love the different theme options.

Fallout Theme

The Fallout series of video games are incredibly popular, and during the game there is a quest and gear activation option, known as the PIP-boy. This is the personal assistant of the character in the game that gives updates on quests, ammunition, health and other data needed. These themes allow you to completely transform your iPad into a portable PIP-boy. This includes the single monotone color scheme, where everything is green, almost like an early 1990s computer screen. You can change the color, if you choose, although you might eventually grow board of the theme. After all, you are spending a good deal of money on the Retina Display on the iPad, so you probably want to show it off with all the different color options available to you.

Install Theme

After you have selected the theme you want and allow it to download to your computer, you now need to install an app from Cydia called Summerboard. This is what changes the theme on the iPad. Allow this to download, and then launch the application. Once there, you are able to select from the list of themes you have downloaded. It takes a bit of time for the device to refresh itself to the new theme, but once it has finished, the entire look and feel of your iPad 3 completely changes to the design and look of the theme you installed on your tablet.

CHAPTER 8- WHAT ARE SOME OF THE KEY FEATURES THAT YOU CAN UNLOCK ON THE IPAD 3?

Features for A Jail Broken IPad 3

With the success that Apple products in today's technological world, it is no question why so many people own an iPad. With the iPad 3 recently being released many people have upgraded to the new model. Now like many cell phone or computer companies applications are usually overpriced and not as beneficial to the user as they promise in the product description. Along with already paying phone and internet bills, apps also require the user to a onetime fee for their use but often leave the user feeling disappointed or angry. This can all be avoided with the use of jail breaking.

Jailbreaking is the ability to access all the hidden features your device can offer you for free. In order to jail break your device you will need to gain permitted control to the operating system of the device. This is not like asking permission though instead you are going to do it anyway. After you gain access to the iPads operating system or iOS, you will be able to install whatever applications you like as well as modifying files to get things to run more efficiently or for ease of access. Now that you know the basics of what jail breaking is we can delve into the reasons why you would even want it attempt it in the first place.

The bread and butter of mobile devices and tablets are the applications that are available on the app stores. These apps can be anything from mind stimulating games, to bar code scanners, and even apps that make your screen look broken so you can give someone a scare especially if a parent or someone has bought you one for a gift. Some of the most rewarding apps however are the ones that are user friendly or allow customization. One such application is Winterboard. With this app, you will be able to customize the whole interface of the device all the way from changing themes for your gadgets, the background to your iPad, and even the original design the application has on your home screen.

When browsing through the app store you may see something that catches your eye but wait, it costs five dollars. Well this is not a problem with Installous.

This application allows the user to browse through a collection of apps from the store and provides you with a link to download the app to your iPad. This is perfect for anyone who does not want that extra charge on the bill for buying an app. If you have ever watched a movie in one display setting then tried to make it full screen and notice those pixels around the edges and are bothered by the stretched quality of the picture will love RetinaPad. While this application does not do this for movies but rather other apps, RetinaPad will display other apps in full screen mode without all the blurriness and rough edges.

Are you either of those people that like everything neat and organized by alphabetized or by genre? Well if you are then MultiIcon Mover is something you will want to download. This application lets you organize all your other apps at once without having to touch and drag them individually. If you have never had a jail broken iPad then you may not know which apps to start downloading right away that could be useful to you without possibly hours of research. Any of these should be able to solve that problem for you.

Having a jail broken iPad does not only limit you to finding great free apps though. Along with applications, you can download what are called tweaks that have more of a user-friendly motive in mind rather than entertainment, which seems to be apps main goal. These however cannot be found in an app store and need to be downloaded elsewhere.

Why not start with Dashboard X, a tweak that allows you to put widgets on the devices springboard. If you are the type of user that uses their iPad to talk to people frequently then try out SwipeSelection. This tweak grants you with a quick and easy way to edit text. This tweak is actually so popular that many users wish it was included as part of the device upon purchase. If the WinterBoard app did not provide you with enough customization then the Springtomize tweak will give you much more than you need. This tweak gives you customization over pretty much everything on your iPad. You will be able to change everything from dock all the way to the notification center. Even if you like to change things everyday for a fresh look this tweak will allow you to get that done with its in depth approach to interface customization.

In today's technological world, everybody is multitasking almost all day especially while browsing the web. With Quasar, you can do that. This tweak runs almost like a computer system on your device. You will be able to multitask while using this. That is great if you are working from home or just really trying to get a couple things at once. If you must have your entire system files organized or managed then iFile will be worth your time. This tweak gives you a very efficient way of doing just that. This tweak can be a very useful to users who are zealous organizers.

These are not the only applications or tweaks you can get for your new iPad, there are many more out there. These are just a few examples to get you started into the world of jail broken devices. More come out with every software update and more often than not, they will always be useful programs. Each of these features will provide the user with something beneficial and leave you feeling satisfied with your files. If any of the features do not stand out to you than simply wait for a new update then browse around until you find something that can help you have the most user-friendly device.

CHAPTER 9- WHAT ARE THE DANGERS OF UNLOCKING OR HACKING YOUR IPAD?

Owning an iPad opens the door to a wide range of abilities. Whether you are looking for something to just surf the web or create stunning documents on, this tablet is the ideal tool for just about everyone. The problem many people run into with the iPad is that the Apple App store is limited in the amount of free apps they offer. If you want a decent app that will be productive for you, then you are likely to spend something to get it. Additionally, there are very few apps that do things to help the system itself as these apps must be done directly through the Apple software or iTunes.

This is why some choose to jailbreak or hack their iPad. When the iPad is jail broken, it has the Cydia application installed. Cydia is an app store that offers various apps to help the system of the iPad as well as offering different productive apps, all for free. As with anything that changes the system of any device, hacking your iPad has its dangers and downsides that can be difficult to get the iPad back to where it was before you attempted the hack. Before any hack, be sure to plug the iPad into a computer and back up all of the important data through iTunes just in case you get it to a point where it a complete restore is required.

No More Software Upgrades

When anything Apple is hacked, it is no longer compatible with the Apple software. When the device is not compatible then it will not accept any software downloads, ever. The Apple software updates fix various bugs and simply keep the device running smoothly. When the device cannot use the update, the device continues to use the same, outdated software and will not allow you to update the software and in some cases, the apps. If you do try and update the software on the iPad after it has been hacked, the iPad will simply lock up during the installation which will make it virtually impossible to get it back to the state it was in before the attempted update. This is often referred to as bricking the iPad. The term brick is used because when a user attempts to do the update on a hacked iPad, it looks and acts like a brick. It will be a heavy piece of metal that has no other use until it has been completely restored.

Crashing Apps

When the iPad is hacked, the standard installed Apple Apps like weather, stocks and even YouTube can become very unstable. If these apps still work, then you are one of the lucky few, on the other hand, when they are still available, they are also said to become very unstable. They crash often and even freeze up the iPad when they are running.

Other apps that push notifications like Gmail and Facebook typically cannot get the information they need to produce the notifications which disrupts the application as well. In essence, hacking an iPad may cause the user to miss important notifications and emails. Additionally, if the iPad is using a 3G or 4G cellular data network that network can become extremely unreliable. This means that unless it is using strictly Wi-Fi, the internet can become extremely unstable with near constant drops in network services.

Low Battery

Another key danger to unlocking an iPad is the battery life. While users often complain about the shortened battery life of a factory iPad, users of unlocked iPads have stated even more that the battery life is even shorter due to the Apple software no longer running in the background and keeping other apps from draining the battery. Now that the iPad is unlocked, any and all apps that can run in the background stays running since the standard operating software is no longer available. With the compromised operating system combined with the constantly running apps, the iPad will likely have a battery life that is greatly reduced.

Risk of Identity Theft

Apple has a reputation of having one of the top security programs in any mobile device. The problem lies when the iPad is jail broken or hacked since it compromises the entire operating system. When the iPad is hacked, it creates holes in the security system which opens the user up to hackers being able to get personal information from social security numbers to credit card numbers as well as passwords to email and social media. Identity theft is one of the most common crimes today which is why Apple has put security measures in place for their operating system. One hack in that system compromises the security of the iPad as well as any user accounts associated with the iPad.

Viruses and Worms Are Back

One thing that all Apple users enjoy is that through the heightened security in the Apple OS which protects devices from various viruses and worms. There are new worms worldwide that are attacking the unlocked iPhones, iPods and iPads. These worms not only create a slow running system but it also opens the user up to a whole new world type of security breach. This breach allows the hacker complete access to everything including contacts, data, applications and even media. When the hacker gets into these files, they can contact anyone in any of your contacts list pretending to be you or even on your behalf in an attempt to run a scam. They can also take any of your credit card numbers and build new cards that they can use virtually anywhere.

If you happen to hack your iPad and you begin to experience any of these problems, you can get the iPad back to its former glory days. All you need to do is to first back up your data through iTunes and then you can restore your iPad back to factory settings. When the restore is complete, it is back to the exact configuration it was when it was first taken out of the box.

CHAPTER 10- TIPS AND HELPFUL HINTS FOR YOUR iPAD

It is basically true that just about anyone can learn to use the iPad at its basic level. This is because the iPad is very basic, so that even 2-year old children can work quite well with it. There really is no actual learning curve, and especially, if you have used an iPhone before, then using an iPad for the first time is a piece of cake. It is just simply made to be that way.

However, even though things have been simplified by Apple for the typical user, there are still some things about iPad use that may take time before you are able to master. Here are a few.

Soft Reset

Apple's iPad can't guarantee that it will perform the same way it did the first time you bought it.

Even though with the iPad there are no moving parts in the device, and although this means the device deteriorates very slowly if at all, there are still some risks that its parts may not work all of the time as they should. This is where the Soft Reset function comes in, just for those situations when the system freezes.

The soft reset is performed by holding the top or power button simultaneously with the front or Home button for a couple of seconds. This will work to force your device to restart. What if you are not happy with how an app is working and need to force quit it? Just hold the Home button the same way, but this time without holding the power button, and the device will exit any running app.

Cut- and Copy-Pasting

Because of how hard it can be to copy long texts on iPad, Apple decided to create an easy solution that will let you copy an entire paragraph without necessary stretching of the blue knobs that appear on the screen. Instead tap any text four times and it will highlight the entire paragraph. However this can only be done if you happen to be copying an editable text. Otherwise, it won't work.

Importing Free eBooks

The iPad can help you get free eBooks for iPad for your iPad reading pleasure.

If you are interested in downloading old books that have fallen out of copyright, you'll find that there is an extensive collection of free eBooks downloadable on iPad. So long as these books are in the public domain such as the classics, you will be happy with free eBooks.

Easy Mute

For those embarrassing moments when you find that you forget to turn off the volume of your multimedia device, you'll find that iPad can come to the rescue. It has an easy mute function that lets you automatically turn the volume off. This way this is done is by pressing the volume down for two seconds and you'll enjoy complete peace and quiet.

Supersized Screenshots

Taking giant screenshots on your iPad is done by holding the power and home buttons simultaneously for half a second.

Bringing the Virtual Keyboard Back

Being able to switch between keyboards – real and virtual keyboards – can now be easy. You only have to hit the eject key on the real, physical keyboard to bring the virtual one up.

CHAPTER 11- SOME COMMON JAILBREAKING TERMS

Absinthe – A GreenpoisOn jailbreak utility used in jailbreaking devices such as the iPhone 4S and iPad 2 and 3. Absinthe got its name due to its connection to GreenPoisOn. It is the name for the rather infamous drink that is green in color and poisonous in high amounts. Like GreenPoisOn, Absinthe is a one-click Jailbreaking solution and lacks some of the advanced features of Jailbeaking tools such as RedSnOw.

Ac1dSnOw – Jailbreak tool that came out in 2011. It was originally released to support a tethered jailbreak for iOS 5

Activator – A jailbreak utility available in Cydia that is used as part of many Cydia tweaks that allow you to assign gestures to bring up applications and utilities. By being able to launch apps, Activator makes it possible for many types of Jailbreak tweaks to work. Most applications will support Activator

BaseBand – Based band is the name given to the modem (radio) firmware, this is part of the device that control the hardware that allows the phone to communicate with the network. It controls the antennae and affects your service and signal. Because of this baseband is very important while unlocking your device, because in changing your baseband, there is the possibility you may fail to unlock the device. If you happened to be happy with your carrier and do not need to unlock, than there is no need to worry about baseband.

BigBoss – One of the biggest, most popular and most maintained of the Cydia sources. It contained a lot of themes, ring tones, wall papers, and sounds an even many Cydia games on it.

BiteSMS – A jailbreak application available in Cydia that also offers users the ability to purchase credits that can be used towards international texting. These credits make it possible to pay less than the carrier rates. BiteSMS is considered a to be a replacement to the built-in Messages application to be found on iPhone and IPod devices.

blackra1n – This is a program used to jailbreak devices that would run versions 3.1, 3.1.1 and 3.1.2 of Apple's operating system for iDevices, also known as iOS.

Blobs – Also called Binary Large Object. Blobs are usually images, audio or other multimedia objects

Bootloader – A piece of code embedded inside an iPhone chip that runs before any iOS is running. It refers to the baseband bootloader and is the code that is run before the baseband firmware. This code is responsible for updating the baseband and signature checking.

Cydia – A software application for the iOS that permits a user to be able to browse and download applications for a jailbroken iPhone, iPad or iPod Touch. Cydia is the software application for iOS that is a graphical front end to APT and the dpkg package management system. Technically speaking, Cydia was the first app store on iPhone. Today, even though Apple has its own apps store, Jailbreakers still use Cydia as app store for Jailbreaking.

DFU – This stands for Device Firmware Upgrade. Many jailbreak software providers require that you put it in this mode when jailbreaking.

DisplayRecorder – Jailbreak utility available in Cydia that allows you to record the display on your iPhone or iPad similar to taking a screen recording on your PC or Mac, since it is equivalent to screencasting software like ScreenFlow.

Dreamboard – New jailbreak app that allows users to easily 'tether' one's mobile device with a USB cable to gain access to the internet. The app, which is currently available in the Cydia Store, is regarded as an acceptable alternative to WinterBoard

Evasi0n – This is the first jailbreak for newer iOS devices such as iPhone 5, iPad mini, iPad 4 and iPod touch 5G.

Greenpois0n – A popular jailbreak utility that helps in jailbreaking your iPhone or iPod Touch and that has been updated several times and can jailbreak multiple versions of iOS.

iOS – A mobile operating system developed and distributed by Apple Inc. It was originally developed for the iPhone, but it has been extended to support other Apple devices such as the iPod Touch, iPad, iPad mini and second-generation Apple TV.

iWipeCache – Clears the cache on iPhone, iPad, and iPod touch. Available in Cydia as a free download. Can also be used to fix the white Cydia icon turning white or even disappearing on iOS 5.0 and above after jailbreaking an iOS device.

limera1n – A jailbreak utility that jailbreaks iPhone 3GS, iPhone 3G, iPhone 4, iPod touch 4th gen, iPad, and AppleTV on certain versions of iOS 3.x and iOS 4.x

MyWi – It's a jailbreak app that lets you tether and even turn an iPhone into a mobile wireless router

My3G – An Application package available in Cydia that allows users to lift many carrier restrictions regarding 3G data such as using FaceTime over 3G.

Redsn0w – This is a free iOS jailbreaking tool developed by the iPhone Dev Team. It can assist in jailbreaks on many iOS devices by using low-level boot ROM exploits along with additional exploits. This is a desktop application that let users jailbreak an iOS device if it is connected to a desktop computer with a standard USB charging cable and is done by clicking a series of buttons. This tool enables the user to have root access on their device and removes Apple's restrictions on installing software outside the App Store.

Springboard – or Home Screen, is the standard application that manages the iOS home screen. In other words, it is the graphical user interface on iOS devices It is like the desktop in a desktop computer.

Tethered Jailbreak – Every time your ipad reboots or loses battery power, it must be attached it to a PC or Mac to get the hardware to boot into the jailbroken state. Tethering is the process by which one iPad or other device shares its Internet connection with another. This happens when one is using a connecting cable or a wireless protocol, such Wi-Fi or Bluetooth. Apple simply chose not to make it directly possible for the iPad to be able to accept an Internet tether from another device. Apple instead intended for the iPad to rely on a direct Wi-Fi connection or the 3G cellular data network

Unlocking – Sometimes the baseband is forced to communicate only with a specific network (Lock to that network). Unlocking is the process of removing, modifying, tricking or working around any carrier restrictions and let the baseband to communicate with any compatible network.

Winterboard – Free download available in Cydia that allows users to theme graphical elements of their SpringBoard. Winterboard isusedto install themes and for customization for the iPad. It allows tweaking and customizing of the smallest details on the springboard.

About The Author

Don Gall was always interested in gadgets so it was only natural that he had an interest in the iPad when it first came on the market. He, just like many other tech heads was intrigued by all the functions that the iPad came with and was interested in figuring out how he could benefit even more from using the device even if it meant entering the world of jailbreaking.

After a while that is exactly what he did and after learning all the cons that come with this process and learning how to effectively avoid he has a device that he gets great service from.

He made the decision to share some of his new found knowledge with others who also have an interest in getting the most out of their device. The tips are outlined in a fashion that is extremely easy to understand and even the individual that is not technologically inclined will have an understanding of what Don has outlined in his book.

The process is pretty simple. The technology will continue to evolve so it is best to catch up as soon as possible so that one does not get left behind the technological wave.

www.ingramcontent.com/pod-product-compliance
Lightning Source LLC
Chambersburg PA
CBHW041145050326
40689CB00001B/490